ANONYMOUS CONSTELLATION

to Rita & Luce

Alfredo de Palchi

Anonymous Constellation

Costellazione Anonima

**Translated from the Italian
by**

Sonia Raiziss

**&
Introduced
by**

Alessandro Vettori

A Xenos Dual-Language Edition

XENOS BOOKS

Library of Congress Cataloging-in-Publication Data

De Palchi, Alfredo 1926–
   [*Anonymous Constellation*. English and Italian]
   Costellazione anonima = Anonymous Constellation / Alfredo de
Palchi, translated from the Italian by Sonia Raiziss and introduced by
Alessandro Vettori.

   p.   cm.
   English and Italian
   "A Xenos dual-language edition."
   ISBN 1–879378–23–X (paper)
   ISBN 1–879378–24–8 (cloth)
   1. De Palchi, Alfredo, 1926– —Translation into English.
   I. Raiziss, Sonia. II. Title. III. Title: *Anonymous Constellation*.

Cover illustration: Watercolor (1994) by Fulvio Testa
Cover photograph: Luca Carrá
Cover design: Kevin Richard
Typesetting: Richard Foerster

Xenos Books
P.O. Box 52152
Riverside, CA 92517-0152

Printed in the United States of America

Acknowledgments

Most of the English versions of these poems were first published in the following journals, and one anthology:

The American Poetry Review
Contemporary Literature in Translation
Gradiva
Granite
The Hampden Sydney Poetry Review
International Poetry Review
Mediterranean Review
Mundus Artium
The Nation
Occum Ridge Review
Paintbrush
Pittsburgh Quarterly
PoliText
Testo a fronte (Milan, Italy)

Italian Poetry Today, anthology edited by Ruth Feldman and Brian Swann (St. Paul, Minnesota, New Rivers Press, 1979)
The original text of 5 appeared in the annual *Almanacco dello specchio, 11* (Milan, Italy, Mondadori Editore, 1983)
The original text of 18 appeared in the chapbook *Mutazioni,* winner of a national literary prize (Udine, Italy, Campanotto Editore, 1988)

I thank Melissa Studdard Williamson and editor/publisher Karl Kvitko for reading and editing the poems and ordering them along an ideal sequence.

Table of Contents

Introduction

Poems of Violence and Dust

Alfredo de Palchi's profound and heartfelt series of reflections on existential matters continues with this new collection of poems, entitled *Anonymous Constellation*. While his previous poetic works—*The Scorpion's Dark Dance* and *Sessions with My Analyst*—reflected on his wartime experience of incarceration and its psychological aftermath, this new collection offers a wider scope for thoughts on human existence in general. With de Palchi reflections are not rare and abstract conceptualizations; they emerge out of the depth of his mind as concrete images, leaping onto the page out of a persisting torment. His terse, unadorned language perfectly suits his poetic images, which proceed by what seem inconsequential analogies, yet are linked by a firm coherence of ideas and concepts underpinning the entire collection. The result is an uninterrupted unity, an organic creation, to be read almost in a single breath.

Anonymous Constellation follows an evolutionary pattern: it starts with iconic refections on primordial cosmic life, proceeds to meditations on human history and ends with statements about the poet himself. Evolution is thus both a theme and a structural element of the collection. But do not expect to find the traditional idea of progress repeated in these pages. De Palchi rejects such a positive construct, whereby a series of incremental, developmental steps perfect creation in the course of time. With bitter irony, he asserts the reverse: that violence levels all creatures and brings them back to their primeval state.

Such a view turns history upside down. History does not instruct; it fails to solve the continuing dilemmas and difficulties of human life. For de Palchi the world is a great struggle—*agon*—in which everyone is at arms against everyone else: human beings against other human beings, human beings against animals, animals against other animals. The poem *Come si può accettare la storia, la storia* ("How can we swallow history, our daily history") raises the question of history's ferocity, here spelled out in ascending stages of development: from insects to mice, to rabbits, to falcons, to people. The evolutionary ladder of cruelty ends with a boy hitting an ox:

> ... *sotto ogni foglia al suolo si appicca*
> *una lotta d'insetti e dovunque*
> *di sopravvivenza: del topo del coniglio*
> *del falco che assalta planando*
> *del ragazzo, beccaio di ferocia allegria*
> *che bastona il bue e con ingordigia di potere*
> *urla ora ti ammazzo.*

> ...under each fallen leaf a war
> of insects and everywhere the rage
> for survival: the mouse the rabbit
> the cruising hawk attack
> and the butcher's boy in his ferocious glee
> lashes the ox and greedy for power
> yells I kill you.

Note that the cruel battle begins under a "fallen leaf," in itself a symbol of declining life. Natural elements in their downward course vent their rage of unfulfillment on their weaker fellows. The ensuing struggles shape the violent path of existence, which people call "history." *Agon* is the occasion for violent clashes of natural beings—animal and human alike. This battling and duelling, intrinsic to existence in all its stages of development, is de Palchi's rendition of the relationship between nature and history, a crucial point around which Western literary tradition revolves. The stronger triumphs over the weaker: such is the fierce natural law depicted in the poem, and by culminating in the cruel boy it wraps the whole of nature into historical turmoil. Thus, as de Palchi's sees it, history has no development. The only channel through which it moves is violence.

The point is stressed in two other poems: *Il triangolo d'alberi* ("Trees and benches, the triangle") and *Nelle cave dei palazzi* ("In the basement of glass buildings"). The first presents a brutal scene in which violence moves in reverse, from human being back down to animal:

il ragazzo malmena il vecchio
il vecchio frantuma una bottiglia
sulla testa del cane
il cane intelligente non scaltro

a kid beats up an old guy
the guy slams a bottle down on the dog's head
the intelligent dog, not cunning

The second poem explains the odd distinction between "intelligence" and "cunning." In making it, de Palchi refers to natural selection, itself a violent, deadly process. He writes:

la paleontologia annulla le menzogne storte
bisogna uccidere e la selezione
espediente non del più forte
o intelligente
ma del più scaltro
decide.

paleontology repeals the distorted lies
there is a need to kill and expedient
selection neither of the strongest
nor the smart:
the most cunning
decides.

If this is the ongoing, unchanging mechanism of earthly existence, then the acquisition of historical knowledge brings no gain to humanity. De Palchi thus brusquely dismisses the time honored concept of the great lives—*historia magistra vitae*. In the poem *La storia nei libri innocua nulla insegna* ("Innocuous history teaches nothing in books"), history is characterized as a cyclical process having no positive lesson for human beings. The poet's conception of history is summed up in the lines: *l'oggi imita l'ieri / e limita il domani* ("today mimics yesterday / and limits tomorrow"). The present imitates the past, thereby creating the cyclical structure of history, which makes the future identical to both past and present. The "imitation" of past historical events is of necessity a "limiting" device, in that it structures the future, and the punning *imita-limita* hints at an organic process, stifling personal and communal creativity. In de Palchi's view, history is synonymous with violence and imitation. Not only is it uninstructive, it is downright destructive. It constitutes an impediment and an encumbrance to one's creativity and spontaneity.

Likewise nature shapes and reshapes itself, only to end up unchanged, caught up in its perverse cyclical pattern of violence and contamination. In the poem *Inarreso l'urto del mare escava macerie* ("The relentless shove of the sea scoops up rubbish"), this pointless progression is depicted iconically with the image of sand on the seashore:

> ... *la sabbia*
> *rimestata da mani imitatrici*
> *della natura che si imita*

> ...sand
> agitated by hands imitating
> nature that mimics itself.

Nevertheless, while the cycle of poems rejects biological nature and human history as negative sides of earthly existence and virtually a parody of themselves, it portrays human nature as an ambiguous mixture of positive and negative components. The poet's definition of himself as an "anonymous constellation" combines these two opposing sides of human nature. "Constellation" conjures up the sublimity of stars and the elevated status of man over beast. However, de Palchi brings us back down to earth by pointing out that the fundamental structuring element of matter, be it above or below, is dust, with all the humility and debasement that such a definition entails. Stars and human beings are two of the infinite number of creatures shaped from dust. As regards that metaphorical constellation called man, the harmonious revolving of the cosmos does not work. Indeed, the poet portrays himself as slightly off-center.

> ... *rigiro su me stesso e spostato di quel tanto*
> *dal mio centro intorno me stesso:*
> *costellazione anonima.*

coiling self-centered and displaced by that much
from my axis, I go round myself:
anonymous constellation.

The same poem begins: *Polvere dovunque su tutto polvere su ciascuno* ("Everywhere dust on all things on all of us dust"). In this context, dust has ambiguous connotations, being at once the cosmic matter at the origin of existence and the mundane stuff of human beings. The poetic parallel both intensifies the archetypal image of original dust and stresses the ambiguity of human nature. The inchoate, lapidary pattern of the collection, with its repeated reference to primordial dust, fulfills de Palchi's "need to trace [his] descent into the inorganic magma, a place of interest to his poetic imagination," as one critic, Rosetta Di Pace Jordan of the University of Oklahoma, put it.

However, once again, de Palchi identifies this "inorganic magma" not with heavenly bodies, but with "mud" and "scum," the shaping matter of human beings. Mankind, in fact, is defined as *fango su due gambe* ("scum on two legs") in order to stress its debased, contaminated nature. This aspect of human nature will not change, de Palchi believes, hence his existential pessimism. People are subject to their inescapable, unchanging destiny, which—exactly like history—runs its course independent of any human effort to divert it. Historical strictures are overcome only when we reach back to find the "inorganic magma" of ourselves and our history. It is then that we will no longer be subject to physical, moral or psychological constraints, nor be dependent on the judgement of others. As we read in *Lo strumento che erode la vita* ("The contraption eroding my life"):

> *forse arriveremo all'origine*
> *al pezzo di terra dove sarò l'indiscreto*
> *giudice di me stesso, non muri*
> *non leggi, tutto aperto:*
> *porte finestre letto*
> *dove nessun altro fango su due gambe giudicherà.*

> perhaps we'll get to the source of it
> a plot of ground where I'll be my own rash

inquisitor, no walls
no laws, everything wide open:
doors windows the bed
where no other scum on two legs shall
judge me.

In sum, the cosmic metaphor of an anonymous constellation captures at once the reference to mythical origins, which we of necessity must recuperate in order to understand our essence, and the debasement and contamination that are a natural, inescapable consequence of human development.

With *Anonymous Constellation,* Alfredo de Palchi has produced another exceptionally original work, distinguished like the preceding by plain and powerful words, startling and disturbing images, and a bold, thought-provoking message.

Alessandro Vettori
University of Virginia

Anonymous Constellation

Pour ce qu'il est tout insensé
—François Villon

Il cerchio rosa cresce in singola
fiamma
      lenta dentro il mattino sempre sterile
sagomando in un taglio la nostra entrata
pieni ancora di sonno
ma già pronti a prendere per il collo
chi è intento a . . . ecco
questo il circolo familiare.

The circle of pink grows in a single
flame
      slow inside the ever-barren morning
shaping the wedge of our re-entry
still logy with sleep
but already set to get a neckhold
on whoever aims to . . . there's
that old familiar cycle.

La decisione d'incontrarmi è dietro
di me, futile, che mai avrò il coraggio
di confrontarmi e mettere a nudo lo spirito quanto
il corpo fedele allo specchio e sputare—
impossibile
          come affrontare la negazione
in me tradita dal mio fallimento.

That resolve to meet myself is squarely
behind me, useless, I'll never have the guts
to confront my identity, strip the spirit naked as I
do the body faithful to the mirror and spit on it—
impossible
            how to face my own denial
betrayed by my failure.

Elencare i fallimenti—
che senso persistere sulla pagina
della inefficienza le ragioni
dell'insuccesso, negoziare uno status quo
per un altro; nessuno
è libero, ognuno soccombe a qualcuno
o qualcosa ed io
stufo d'una vita squattrinata mi concedo
una ricchezza ben diversa:
                                    chi mi suppone
in ginocchio alla fioritura pulsante vede
pure che le mangio la vita.

I wish to list my failures—
the sense to persist on the page
of inefficiency the causes
of my flop, to negotiate a status quo
for another; nobody
is free, all succumb to somebody
or something and fed-up
with a pennyless life I grant myself
a very different wealth:
                    who imagines me
knee-bent and bowed, before the pulsating bulb,
can see I'm also eating its life.

Penso alle assuefazioni ai dinamismi
integrali
come si congiura per esistere—
congiuro contro me stesso
e ascolto i fatti
le narrazioni olfattive i difetti
abbelliti di parole
e il centrifugo tracciare la consuetudine.

I think of the ways of habit of essential
energies
how we plot to exist—
I plot against myself
and listen to the facts
the tales I smell out the defects
embellished with words
and the centrifugal tracking of custom.

Questo il significato:
la sinistra indulgenza che mi scabbia
la pelle e pesta un pudore
evanescente è la terza conseguenza
del malessere di quarantenne,
è la giovinezza persa
l'altro ieri tramite la scossa della realtà
solo considerata nel subconscio ed evitata:
può un altro bastardo meglio definirmi?

This is what I mean:
the sinister indulgence that scars
my skin and crushes a fading
decency, is the third stage of a man's
malaise at 40
is youth lost
just yesterday shocked by a reality that only
the subconscious admits then shuns:
can some other bastard define me better?

Nessuna certezza
dalla spiritualità arcaica del mare—
gesticolo le braccia al cielo che affonda
sbilanciato nei verdi avvallamenti

mutazione cosciente
vescica rovesciata metamorfosi
per un abisso d'alghe e pesci,
non mi differenzio—sono
l'escrescenza che si lavora in questa
epoca
          e dovunque bocche di pesci
          aguzze su altri pesci

il mare un vasto cratere—
e fissi al remoto i pesci graffiti
non guizzano dove sradicato
il gabbiano è l'unica dimensione
conscia
          dell'inarrivabile bagliore.

Nothing certain
rises from the spiritual archaic seas—
my arms gesture to the skies foundering
off-balance in the green caves of valleys

conscious mutation
vesicle pulled inside out, metamorphoses,
through chasms of algae and fish,
not that I'm different—being
the excrescence working in this same
epoch
          and everywhere the maws of fishes
          sharpens on others

the sea an immense crater—
and fish graffiti fixed on distance
don't dart where now the uprooted
gull is the only
dimension aware of
          that still unattainable flash.

Domani un altro giorno, non sole
solo il cielo immediato
elettrico di atmosfera che . . .
non devo soccombere
alla pecunaria esistenza
deteriorare—qualcuno qualcosa
mi riabiliterà ma non c'è prospetto:

ho preso una strada
per un'altra, incontro gente che non capisco
e non capisce / come portare un fagotto
sulla schiena è la gioia / perché
temere quella strada /
sono un bastardo che si gratta le pulci /
il dominio del cuore è soggetto
femminile / e non dimentico
che nessuno mi ha crocifisso
ma io stesso.

Tomorrow is another day, there's no sun
only the sky is close
electric with an aura that . . .
I mustn't succumb
to my penniless existence
or let it get worse—somebody something
will redeem me but there's no prospect:

I mistook one road
for another, I meet people I don't know
who don't understand / how to carry a pack on my back
is the joy of it / why
dread that road /
I'm a mutt who scratches at his fleas /
domain of the heart is a woman's
topic / and I don't forget that
nobody
crossed me but myself.

La Cristianità di che succede
è un seguito di fatti
pedagogici e di turbolenze
simbolo di quella vita più nascosta
dell'atomo
   —che dire che fare allora
per scoprire la prova esatta e chiarirla
al girasole che respira col mollusco
asse magnetico
ora qui a metà vita, o udire
ciò che non vorrei apprendere o ammettere
fra un miscuglio incongruo di oggetti
di gente senza direzione
che precisi i punti di 'partenza' 'arrivo'
e viene da una porta e va all'altra formando
una cerchia d'intrusione
ed ammassa una roccia
di collera nel ventre e vulnera
la pera del cuore crepato dal verme che scava
con logica quello che rimarrà per sempe assente.

The Christian thing of what happens
is a chain of school
facts and commotions
symbol of that life
more secret than the atom
        —what's there to say then or do
to find the true test and explain it
to the sunflower breathing with the mollusc
magnetic axis
now just midway in life or hearing
what I'd rather not learn or concede
among an incongruous jumble of
objects directionless people
who define the points of "departure," "arrival"
come in one door and go out another creating
a circle of intrusion
that heaps my belly with a rock
of wrath and wounds the heart's pear
split by the worm digging
methodically at what remains forever absent.

Ritenendo che una vita vale un'altra
nel mio laboratorio combino alchimie contro
leggi della scienza e natura:
asserita visione della insolente legge
del vano aguzzino vistoso
soggiogato alla propria alienazione;
se mi lascio fare e parlare
riesco a pormi al muro
e annullarmi / bianco delitto
prendimi a calci, buttami nel fondo
della vampa e staziona il presente
incolume alle origini.

Finding one life worth another
in my lab I mix alchemies against
the laws of science and nature:
confirmed vision of the impudent law
of man, flashy cruel empty
subject of his own alienation;
if I let go and talk
I'd stand up at the wall
and rub myself out / innocent crime
kick me and hurl me to the pit
of the fire and leave the present
unhurt at its beginnings.

In Times Square fra spacchi di neon
snervanti muraglie e rombo
di veicoli le passioni
adulterate—dove
sostare: in un bar
che alimenta sesso insonnia
e manie.

In Times Square between daggers of neon
exhausted walls and growling
traffic steam the corrupted
passions—I look for a
break: in a bar? of course,
that spoonfeeds you sex insomnia and
obsessions.

Il terrore di essere là quando è l'ora
di rinascere a ritroso poco
a poco come
è dentro nel lavoro nella paga
a fine settimana
con il debito da pagare definitivo
certo senza passione nel corpo
definito   bloccato

The terror of being there in the hour
of rebirth receding little
by little
as it goes, through work through wages
at the end of the week
with one definitive debt to settle for sure
dispassionately in the body
defined   blocked

Il fracasso dietro quei muri accesi
quei blocchi verticali
lorda la mia esistenza che si chiude
breve nella propria luce
ed in unisono con gli animali che sono
la somiglianza
di quello che io
sono.

The clamor behind those lighted walls
those vertical blocks
dirties my life that shuts up
short in its own shining
and in harmony with the animals which are
the likeness
of what I
am.

Sono
     —questo il punto/idea connettivo—
l'unto dell'acqua l'insettivoro petrolio
sigillato da eruzioni
pozzi sotto il fondale, l'oceano grasso
di corpuscoli, plancton che funziona
con premura per i crostacei
per il pesce cui serve ad altro pesce
e avanti secondo l'inevitabile alimento
e grossezza—coriaceo predatore, secco
rogo di pinne dorsali e pettorali
su peduncoli o trampoli
da suggerire tracce di membra
e la spina un tubo
di cartilagine: il coelacanth
non estinto.

I am
      —here's the point/connecting idea—
watery grease insectivorous oil
sealed by eruptions
wells under the bottom, the ocean fat
with corpuscles, plankton
functioning with zeal for crustaceans
for fish serving other fish and so on
and so on according to size and the inexorable
food chain—tough predator, dry
fire of dorsal and pectoral fins
erect on pedicles or stilts
implying traces of limbs and the spine
a gristly tube: the coelacanth
not yet extinct.

Al finestrino guizza il mondo—
ancora fa nero e piano
il cielo crescente si chiazza,
tutto è sterile, astringente:
case / cespugli / alberi stecchiti
animali sbudellati lungo l'autostrada e noi
che ci odiamo accalcati nella corriera.

È un mondo breve composto, simbolo atroce
di quello fuori . . . schiavi della meschina
esistenza, ammutoliti e restii a dire
buongiorno, siamo
manichini col motore al culo.

The world's a flash in the window—
it's still dark, a gradual
sky widens, stains with dawn
all is sterile astringent:
houses / bushes / starved trees
animals on the freeway gutted by wheels
and us hating each other jammed in the bus.

It's a proper brief world, odious symbol
of that big one outside . . . we're tools of a wretched
life, tongue-tied and dreading to say
hi there, nothing
but manikins with a motor in our tails.

Che pazienza
ascoltare il mentale pertugio di lagne:
oscena concordia di affaristi, teste
aggressive ficcate nel cappelluccio: una scena
di scemi ma più drammatica
perché da deridere—
                              no, mi propello
sulla bellezza anche astratta, oltre
quella putrefazione di carne esangue,
e trovo lo stesso il mondo
un inginocchiatoio: calamità – grida
armi – soldi – armi

What patience it takes
to listen to the groans of small minds:
obscene chorus of businessmen, bullish
heads buried in little hats: a scene
of cretins so solemn
you have to laugh—

                      no, I jump
at beauty even in the abstract
beyond that rotting of bloodless flesh,
and still I find the world
on its kneeling-stool: disaster – howls
arms – money – arms

Cancellami
quando neanche si respira quando
neanche si ascolta il piano
fumando bevendo e magari chiavando—
è luogo comune
dovunque noia carenza
di uno spirito che tutto dovrebbe smuovere
nella carne scentrata: potrei anch'io
guarire del cancro che siamo
fossi un luogo comune.

Count me out
when you can neither breathe
nor listen to the piano
while having a smoke a drink and maybe a fuck—
it's so commonplace
everywhere boredom failure
of a spirit that could shake things up
in the displaced flesh: even I could be
cured of the cancer we are
were I that ordinary.

Al mutare delle età spingo
ad altre terre
il mio senza ritorno
e chiedo quale via
al cuore che a istinto d'uccello
m'indica la direzione.

At the changing of the ages I veer off
towards other worlds
to a point of no return
and ask my heart
with its bird's instinct
to show me the way.

L'insettivoro incendio allo zero
compila un miasma—afrore di cadute
nel pugno visibile mette insetti
—io
l'incendio che brulica la specie
spermatozoi
come la mantide predatrice
che progenita divorando.

The insect-eating fire shrinks
a miasma down to zero—the stench of ruin
lays insects in the visible fist
—I
am the blaze where the species swarms
the spermatozoa
like the "preying" mantis
begetting devouring.

Polvere dovunque su tutto polvere su ciascuno
su me un cadere continuo di polvere dal soffitto
sul letto tappeti bottiglie dalle pareti
che mi serrano nella morsa del mio futuro cadavere
già sepolto sotto il cumulo di polvere di questa
polvere che rassodata nello spazio gira su sé stessa
e intorno il sistema termonucleare come me cadavere
che rigiro su me stesso e spostato di quel tanto
dal mio centro intorno me stesso:
costellazione anonima.

Everywhere dust on all things on all of us dust
on me a continuous drizzle of dust from the ceiling
covering the bed carpets bottles
from walls which lock me in the vise of my future
cadaver already buried under the cumulus of dust this
dust that curdles in space, spins round itself
round the thermonuclear system a cadaver like me
coiling self-centered and displaced by that much
from my axis, I go round myself:
anonymous constellation.

Pila di neve sulla città informe
arcata cadaverica
con incertezze di macchie, il selciato
nero, ruote ingranate
fumo di benzina solido
e melma di sale su cui si affanna
il becco della fame
                    —la neve cresce
solidifica raggiere di piume
strappate ai voli / e il gelo uno
a uno uncina gli animali
canditi e il sale aguzzo li sconsacra
polpa maciullata piumaggio pelle.

Snow drifts over the shapeless city
cadaverous arcade
with vague blotches, the pavement
tarred black, wheels locked in gear
dense gas fumes and
salted mud where hungry beaks
worry and dig
                    —the snow swarms
congeals halos of feathers
sheared off in flight / and one
by one the frost hooks the animals
in aspic, salt barbs profane them
crushed pulp plumage skin.

La neve che alla porta si asfalta di ghiaccio
bilancia la potenza della mente, poi
acqua concorre a soffocare o alimentare
quello che ancora si muove:
cane pianta talpa
l'erba corta e zeppa di bruciato

in questo ambiente di taccagni fissi al vetro
a spiare sganasciandosi a vuoto
noto l'umanità sdentata repellente scema
infatuata alla TV
sesso malmenato e la mente desolata
quanto la certezza della neve.

The snow at the door that turns into icy asphalt
holds the balance of power in the mind, then
water conspires to smother or feed
whatever still moves:
dog plant mole
the grass cropped and calked by the cold burn

in this environment of misers glued to the windows
spying on the street, vacantly chomping,
I note humanity toothless repulsive
infatuated halfwit at the TV screen
sex abused
and mind as surely desolate as snow.

Questa neve m'indietreggia
verso l'ostacolo che ero: ogni cosa
efficienza timidezza gente
è ancora ostacolo paranoico

                      —la coscienza
gentile animale braccato che si spacca a mezzo
come coinvolgerla possederla nella melma
di carne / il mio mondo
in cataclismi perpetui si piega
nel proprio asse rotatorio cambiando luogo di clima
seppellendo vita e scoprendo
l'essenza che si spacca a mezzo contro il muro
della coscienza.

This snow pushes me back
towards the obstacle I once was: everything
competence diffidence people
still stands as a paranoid block

                              —conscience
that tender beast at bay rending itself in two
how to involve it possess it in the murk
of flesh / my world
twists in perpetual cataclysms
on its rotary axis exchanging climate
burying life and disclosing
an essence that breaks in half against the wall
of my conscience.

Lo strumento che erode la vita
è il surplus che conviene a me
sottoscritto alla forza—
non dimenticare,
forse arriveremo all'origine
al pezzo di terra dove sarò l'indiscreto
giudice di me stesso, non muri
non leggi, tutto aperto,
porte finestre letto,
dove nessun altro fango su due gambe
giudicherà.

The contraption eroding my life
is the surplus which suits me fine
conscripted under pressure—
remember,
perhaps we'll get to the source of it
a plot of ground where I'll be my own rash
inquisitor, no walls
no laws, everything wide open,
doors windows the bed,
where no other scum on two legs shall
judge me.

È che imbianco l'esistenza
con il lavoro
        e con il soldo pronto
a saldare ogni mese le fatture dei misfatti
a puntellare i debiti con la bruttura costante
e poi vedere
quasi sentire che in me la bellezza
c'è e intorno al mattino—
che continui così continui
perché io stia in piedi davanti
a tante sberle di facce.

It's that I blank out existence
with work
        and keep some ready cash
to settle the monthly bills for small crimes
to shore up debts with their hideous habit
and then see
almost sense the glory inside me
and round me in the morning—
may it go on like this go on
so I may stand up to
all those faces that beg to be slapped.

Hanno sparato il negro
in un negozio di erbivendoli,
frizzante la testa di crespo
poggia in una cassetta
di pomidoro
        – Ha rubato soldi dalla cassa –
borbotta la calca ed io intuisco
nella tasca di chiunque
l'indice lesto sul grilletto.

Scrollo le spalle che mi fanno male
pensando al cozzo nelle sue e alla faccia
di scarnati pomidoro
        – È sangue? –
        – Eh, è un nigger –
osserva un bagonghi.

They shot a black man
in a fruit store,
his tingling crinkled head
lands in a crate
of tomatoes
          – He grabbed some money from the till –
the crowd grumbles and I sense
some guy's trigger-happy
finger in his pocket.

I shrug my shoulders, hurting at the thought
of the crash in his own and at the sight of his face
tinged with busted tomatoes
          – Is that blood? –
          – Eh, he's just a nigger –
says a dwarf clown.

Il senso di che si aspetta
o dell'inaspettato
—il mondo sorride sotto il pugno
noi abbiamo scelto di non piangere non
aiutare ma guardare altrove
quando s'incontra il tramortito
e di passare con l'indifferenza
che si ha per l'animale travolto
dalla macchina o dall'arma—
è inutile pretendere, ognuno
è per sé stesso
e sta in sé stesso.

The meaning of what we expect
or the unexpected
—the world grins under a fist
we have opted for not weeping not helping
but looking away
when a body collapses
and walking off with the same indifference
we feel for the beast knocked out
by a car or a shotgun—
it's useless to pretend, everyone
is out for himself
and locked in himself.

Perché allora rimpiangere quello che è
e non è stato
o illudermi di una vita che non è quella
che sarebbe dovuta e dovrebbe
essere / già il fallimento
scende al nadir / non c'è ricupero
un ricominciare daccapo,
il risultato finale era
all'inizio
            —adottato dalla bruttura
e violenza ora
la collera della mia età è uno strappo
di vesti / è l'essenza
entro me lacerato.

Then why regret what was
and was not
or delude myself with a life which never
could but
should have been / already failure
spirals to its nadir / there's no rescue
no beginning anew,
the end result was there
at the start
          —adopted child of squalor
and violence now
the rage of my times is tearing
its clothes / it's the essence
inside my lacerated self.

E ciò che consideri cuore è un bulbo
non ancora artificiale; lo sarà un giorno
e non racchiuderà menzogne—
meglio anche per me, meno miseria,
cosí fuori luogo, troppo per consolidarmi nel peso
enorme dell'odio, io
poter sparire con lo spirito
forte deciso
e in mano un'arma che mi termini qui
in mezzo il letame umano
buono per bruciare la decenza.

And what you consider a heart is a bulb
not yet artificial, as it will be one day
and it won't hold lies—
better even for me, less misery,
so out of place I can't take root in the huge
weight of loathing, I
to be able to let go, resolved
in mind
and gun in hand to finish me off here
in the middle of manshit
perfect for the burning of decency.

Come si può accettare la storia, la storia
quotidiana, assuefarsi ai grandi e piccoli
insulti—sotto ogni foglia al suolo si appicca
una lotta d'insetti e dovunque
di sopravvivenza: del topo del coniglio
del falco che assalta planando
del ragazzo beccaio di ferocia allegria
che bastona il bue e con ingordigia di potere
urla ora ti ammazzo.

How can we swallow history, our
daily story, get used to enormous and petty
insults—under each fallen leaf a war
of insects and everywhere the rage
for survival: the mouse the rabbit
the cruising hawk attack
and the butcher's boy in his ferocious glee
lashing the ox and hungry for power
yells now I kill you.

La storia nei libri innocua nulla
insegna e nulla imparo dalle esterne vicende
rifacimenti d'interiori
conseguenze
                    l'oggi imita l'ieri
e limita il domani—che importa
vi è sempre scempio
o altra pulizia altra sicurezza
altro esempio

l'acqua riflette su ogni evento anche
il meno plausibile
e il più lurido fiume stagno
superficie scivolosa di schiuma verde
in sé concentra la nettezza
concentrica
del passero zampe aggrappate al filtro
del buco—ad ali stese pare spicchi
il volo ma staccarlo
è un peso annegato di sete.

Innocuous history teaches nothing
in books and I learn nothing from external events
reenactments of interior
issues
            today mimics yesterday
and limits tomorrow—what does it matter
there's always carnage
or another cleanup, some other assurance
a different example

water reflects on every event, even
the least plausible
and the dirtiest river the shallow
pool, slithering surface of green scum
sucks into itself the sparrow's
concentric
terseness his claws hooked to the drainhole
—with stretched wings as if for
flight but the take-off
is weight drowning of thirst.

Nelle cave dei palazzi di vetro macchine
per lavare, turbine
garages—la città è il generatore per ogni servizio
sedia elettrica / non si deve
uccidere contro natura /
non è vero:
la paleontologia annulla le menzogne storte
bisogna uccidere e la selezione
espediente non del più forte
o intelligente
ma del più scaltro
decide.

In the basement of glass buildings the washing
machines, turbines
garages—the city generates every service
the electric chair / we must not
kill against nature /
that's not true:
paleontology repeals the distorted lies
there is a need to kill and expedient
selection neither of the strongest
nor the smart:
the most cunning
decides.

La diga che crolla affascina quanto
il soldato in elmetto e fasciato di bende
frana ai propri piedi
e fuori dei sotterfugi—è l'inutile
Cristo ammucchiato sul terreno
da non difendere o cane da guardia
sul terrapieno dell'artificio

L'ingegnere sa più del soldato
e delle preghiere del prete quando
acqua e melma esplodono
giù piante bestie case ricreando
drammatiche statue di terra fredda.

The collapsed dam fascinates like the
soldier, helmet on head swaddled in bandages
crumpling to his heels
and out of make-believe—this useless
Christ huddled on a field
not to be defended nor
any watchdog on the earthworks

the engineer knows more than the soldier
the chaplain's prayers when
mud and water explode downward
trees animals houses creating
theatrical statues of cold clay.

La distruzione totale è uno scopo
coerente—
                    poter calare nel centro
della terra una forza solare di megatoni
o meglio
svegliare un mattino estinto
d'ogni specie e godere l'ansia in terrore
dell'uomo che si caccia per pasto:
non è odio / è giusta coerenza.

Total destruction is its own consistent
end
                    power to ram into the earth's guts
a solar force of megatons
or better still
to wake one morning empty of
other species and enjoy man
hunting man for his food:
it's not hate / it's proper
consistency.

Il triangolo d'alberi e panchine
tra le due vie è battaglia demente

di notte sempre di notte—luce
è invenzione—il ragazzo malmena un vecchio
il vecchio frantuma una bottiglia
sulla testa del cane:
il cane intelligente, non scaltro,
in agonia conosce finalmente le due
facce
      osservando e operando
      s'impara l'alienazione
      leggo in una latrina

Trees and benches, the triangle
between two streets is an insane battlescene

at night always at night—light
is its own invention—a kid beats up an old guy
the guy slams a bottle down
on the dog's head:
intelligent, not cunning,
the dog in his agony knows the two
faces at last
        observing and acting
        we learn about madness
        this I read in the john

Lo scuro dell'albero che implora luce
s'addensa e macchia il cielo basso di pioggia
con valanghe di sporcizia
                              —l'albero si affanna
si contorce ora come un gigante
animale avvelenato
e qui io un altro albero dilaniato mi contorco
risentito di essere
uomo.

The gloom of the tree imploring light
gathers and blots with mudslide
the sky sagging with rain
                              —the anxious tree
contorts now to a great
poisoned beast
and here another ruined tree
I twist resentful for being
human.

Non violare
il mio fiore di nascita
è già nel tempo / altro
deve arrivare / non so vivere /
/ ho perduto /
lascio che tutto rotoli
giù
finché non c'è più discesa.

Don't profane
the bloom of my birth
already set in its time / something else
must happen / unable to live /
/ I've lost out /
I let it all roll
down
till there's no more falling.

La notizia è questa:
chiuso tutto, nessuno capisce
niente e nessuno—il silenzio
che è voce contamina l'altra voce
e la parola che si spinge fuori
non ha senso
è morte vivente in noi:
un tubo di terrore.

This is the news:
a total shutdown, nobody understands
nothing and no one—silence,
which is voice, contaminates the other
voice and the word pushing through
makes no sense—
it's death alive in us:
a tube of terror.

Giganti acciai inossidabili
si spingono al vuoto dove il saldatore
mani grosse dal guanto la paga
si misura con la fiamma
—sotto l'elmetto
e la maschera
la mente stretta sta
zitta.

Gigantic steel rods
plunge into the void where the welder
with huge gloves for hands
gets paid by the vomit of each flame
—under his helmet
and mask
the clamped mind stays
silent.

Le paradossali vicende sciocche del cuore
le tentazioni organiche del plasma
pompano quest'uomo dimezzato
scentrato da persone diverse entro
una: anomala forma
d'una esistenza di continuo incompiuta
termina qui—il resto
che ricevo e dono non è che apparenza
o interesse.

The heart's silly paradoxical events
the organic temptations of the blood
pump this split man
off-centered by different persons
within one: anomalous life-form
continuously unfinished and
ending right here—the rest
I get and give is nothing by appearance
or self-interest.

Acquistare voce
è assurdo quanto la conquista di conchiudere
una nascita un certificato di padre

come giustificare l'assenza di un padre
e il bisogno di restare assente ora
e nel futuro che affievolisce,
spostare lo stato di questa
insicurezza
incrocio di sventure e gioia stupenda
nel magma di passività / calcolare
e cancellare quello che è stato
è e sarà.

To claim my voice
is absurd like winning a decree
of birth, a father's certificate

how justify the absence of a father
and my need to stay absent now
and in the future that grows faint
to alter the state of this
uncertainty
a crossing of misfortune with stunning joy
in the magma of stagnation / to calculate
and cancel whatever has been
is and will be.

Brulica la spiaggia
si condensa di cicche, fumetti
carta velina unta, ossi succhiati di pollo
mezi panini bottiglie lattine
centinaia di canestri vuoti

i fiori catarrali di sputi
le infiammabili macchie di pelle nera
il gergo volgare e l'immensa vecchia flaccidezza
mi ricordano stupendi
roghi di benzina.

The swarming beach
curdles with cigarette butts, comics
greasy waxpaper, sucked chickenbones
half-eaten rolls bottles tincans
hundreds of trashbaskets, empty

catarrhal flowers of spit
flammable patches of black skin
vulgar jargon and mountains of old flab
how they conjure up
huge gasoline pyres.

Inarreso l'urto del mare escava macerie
resti da decifrare
legni, ossi paleolitici
epoche di screpolature e friabile argilla
che s'impone
                    così urta questa
                    oltre i legni / gli ossi / la sabbia
                    rimestata da mani imitatrici
                    della natura che si imita.

The relentless shove of the sea scoops up rubbish
scraps for deciphering
wood, paleolithic bones
epochs of fissures and brittle
pressures of clay
                    so all this collides
                    beyond wood / bones / sand
                    agitated by hands imitating
                    nature that mimics itself.

Vergogna, io? di questa tridimensionale
vita che mi mena di ruota
in sedia e viceversa,
che compie scempiaggini giorno
dopo giorno sempre più breve
bestemmiato dal mio disdegno e che si oscura
in un lavoro di demolizione—oltre questo
non uno spiraglio di luce ma una corsia
ininterrotta di uomini che si aggirano:
la fortuna è di resistere questi volti
imprecisi

non vi è esito, sono
una catena di subdole origini
ordigni ordini fantasie
che posseggono già l'estinzione
una poltiglia di fango, un fastidioso silenzio
sulla brace di chi ancora vive—
io / che assisto al crescendo d'ogni alba /
alla sera non sono che il semplice
shock dei due estremi.

Who me, ashamed? of this three-dimensional
life that shuttles me from chair to
wheels and vice versa
completing its absurdities day
after day ever shorter
cursed by my disdain and darkening
in the work of demolition—beyond all this
there's no shaft of light but an unbroken
passage of wandering men:
it's my luck to resist these vague
faces

there's no way out,
I'm a chain of insidious origins
orders mechanisms fantasies
already charged with extinction
gruel mud, tedious hush
laid on the coals of the still living—
I / witness of each morning's crescendo /
am nothing at evening but the simple
shock of two extremes.

Un frastuono di ferraglia alle finestre—
i vetri strepitano e scintillano
e gli alberi della piazza scossi dall'autunno
buttano via lo scintillìo

                    come io scosso mi spoglio
della tensione che spunterà da sotto la neve
di nuovi semi il prossimo
aprile.

A metallic racket at the windows—
the glass rattles and sparkles
and the trees of the square in autumnal quakes
shake off their glitter
                              as I strip off
the tension which from under the snow will sprout
with new seeds next
April.

Concepire l'assoluto naufragio che alla superficie
non rimandi ritagli di vita
ormai altrove

———————————————

niente in vista
         eccetto il puntiglio rozzo
nella corrente non ortodossa—
l'indicazione è giusta
ma la forza dell'errore compulsivo
mi afferma
per la controcorrente che conferma statica
la posizione finché la mia totalità
si esaurisce contro quella immune forza.

Imagine a total shipwreck that casts on the surface
no fragments of a life
already elsewhere

———————————

nothing in view
              only the rough particulars
in the unorthodox current—
the signs are right
but the force of the compulsive blunder
affirms me
through the opposing tide that confirms the point
of inertia till my whole self
is exhausted against that immune power.

Desistere dai mezzi termini—
                              la condanna
è di soggiogare e amare con le viscere
nutrire la vampa dell'odio
accerchiare il limite e spaziare
l'essere astratto che spinge
spinge dentro la muraglia di carne esplosioni
le intensità estranee
a cui partecipo per concepirmi e dar loro
una plausibile concretezza.

Give up halfway measures—

                         the verdict:
to subdue, to love with one's guts
to feed the blaze of hatred
to surround my own limits
and space out the abstract creature pushing
pushing inside the walls of flesh eruptions
alien intensities
which I share to renew myself and
lend them a plausible concreteness.

Un ritorno sicuro dove il primo seme
mi chiude una volta gli occhi
per riaprirli su te—
nella polvere il sangue si coagula e indietreggia
alla nascita

fioriscila con la tua, emergila
dal sottosuolo di rottami
e dal crescere di omuncoli
che si divinizzano allo specchio vero
offuscato dalla mente subdola
per oscurare l'altra verità.

A safe return to where the first seed
had once closed my eyes
to open them again on you—
my blood curdles in the dust
and falls back to my birth

make it flower with yours
lift it up from the underground of rubbish
scrubgrowth of homunculi
seeing themselves divine in the true mirror
smeared by the shifty mind
to obscure the other truth.

Alfredo de Palchi

Translations of modern Italian poets in the *Atlantic Monthly, The Quarterly Review of Literature, Poetry, The Virginia Quarterly Review*, and *Eugenio Montale: Selected Poems* (New Directions: New York, 1965).

His own poetry has appeared in various journals, including *The American Poetry Review, Chicago Review, The Massachusetts Review, Mundus Artium, New Letters*, and *TriQuarterly*.

Co-editor with Sonia Raiziss of the Italian section of *Modern European Poetry* (Bantam Books: New York, 1966).

Sessioni con l'analista (Arnoldo Mondadori Editore: Milan, 1967).

Sessions with My Analyst. Translated by I.L. Salomon (October House: New York/London, 1970).

Mutazioni (Campanotto Editore: Udine, 1988).

The Scorpion's Dark Dance. Translated by Sonia Raiziss (Xenos Books: Riverside, CA, 1993; second revised edition, 1995).

Senior associate editor, *Chelsea*.

Sonia Raiziss

Her own poetry and translations from the Italian appeared in many journals.

Through a Glass Darkly (Editions du Phare: Paris).

La poésie américaine "moderniste" 1910-1940 (Mercure de France: Paris, 1948).

The Metaphysical Passion: Seven Modern Poets and the Seventeenth Century Tradition (University of Pennsylvania Press, 1952; reprinted by Greenwood Press: Westport, CT, 1977).

Editor, Italian section of *Modern European Poetry* (Bantam Books: New York, 1966).

Bucks County Blues (New Rivers Press: St.Paul, MN, 1977).

Translation from the Italian: *The Scorpion's Dark Dance* by Alfredo de Palchi (Xenos Books: Riverside, CA, 1993).